Mental Maths 3

Anita Straker

CAMBRIDGE
UNIVERSITY PRESS

1a

1	86 – 50.	**6**	12 minus 8, plus 7.
2	Divide 120 by 10.	**7**	Find the product of 3 and 9.
3	Five threes.	**8**	Take £3.75 from £5.
4	Subtract 12 from 30.	**9**	6×10.
5	47 + 9.	**10**	How many 50p coins make £9?

1b

1 How many right angles can you see altogether?

2 What unit would you use to weigh a snail?

3 Write in order, smallest first: 2012, 1022, 1202.

4 What do twelve 10p coins total?

5 What fraction of this circle is shaded?

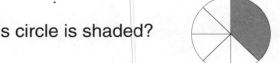

6 Find the cost of 100 crayons at 6p each.

7 What is the value of the 2 in 2070?

8 Egg boxes hold 6 eggs.
How many boxes are needed for 40 eggs?

9 How many millimetres is one centimetre?

10 Roughly how tall is your front door:
2 m, 4 m or 6 m?

c

Copy the diagram.

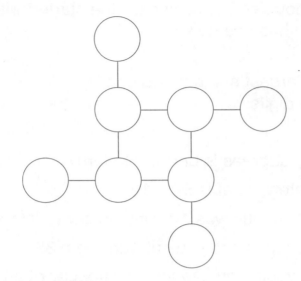

Use each of the numbers 1 to 8.
Write one number in every circle.

Each line of three numbers must add up to 12.

1 2 3 4 5 6 7 8

d

1	58 + 6.	**6**	One tenth of 400.
2	Six threes.	**7**	42 × 10.
3	Add 3, 4 and 5.	**8**	How many corners has a cube?
4	46 + 10.	**9**	15 take away 8, add 9.
5	12 × 0.	**10**	17 plus 5 minus 9.

3

2a

1   Write **two thousand and seventeen** in figures.

2   Mira has doubled her savings. She started with 75p. How much has she now?

3   Make the largest number you can with these digits.

4   How many degrees is one whole turn?

5   Approximately, what is 59 + 19?

6   The 3:05 p.m. bus was 10 minutes early. What time did it come?

7   How many times can you cut 4 cm from 35 cm of ribbon?

8   What unit would you use for the capacity of a tablespoon?

9   What is half way between 36 and 44?

10   Roughly, what does an egg weigh: 50 g, 250 g or 500 g?

2b

1   172 − 60.

2   5 × 20.

3   91 − 7.

4   6 × 5.

5   28 + 4.

6   How many 2p coins make £1?

7   One tenth of £5.

8   351 × 10.

9   Double 34.

10   28 ÷ 4.

1	15 + 9.	**6**	Three tenths of 50p.
2	2 × □ = 18.	**7**	201 – 2.
3	670 × 10.	**8**	99 + 3.
4	33 – 7.	**9**	Eight fours.
5	132 + 20.	**10**	How many 20p coins make £6?

2d

Copy the diagram.

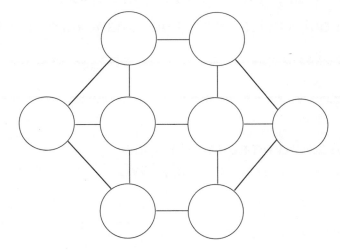

Use each of the numbers 1 to 8.
Write one number in every circle.

Numbers joined by lines must differ by at least 2.

Do it in at least two different ways.

1 2 3 4 5 6 7 8

3a

1. How many days in 5 weeks?

2. What is the value of the 3 in 6732?

3. Round 48.7 to the nearest whole number.

4. Does my eggcup hold 5 ml, 50 ml or 500 ml?

5. Which three of these add up to 13?

6. Write 3.68 metres in centimetres.

7. What unit would you use to measure the length of a river?

8. How many right angles are two full turns?

9. How many pairs can be made from 25 socks?

10. 8 km is about 5 miles. About how many miles is 4 km?

3b

Copy the crossword on squared paper.
Write the answers in words: ONE, TWO, THREE …

Across

1. Half of 30.

4. $3 \times \square = 33$

5. $51 - 49$.

7. $140 \div 14$.

Down

2. $98 - 78$

3. $27 \div 3$.

4. One quarter of 32.

6. 9 plus 6, minus two 7s.

3c

1   Write **five thousand and seventy** in figures.

2   3 pears cost the same as 5 apples.
     Which is cheaper: an apple or a pear?

3   4 children can sit at a table.
     How many tables are needed for 29 children?

4   Winston spent £6.50 in one shop and £9 in another.
     How much did he spend altogether?

5   14 fives make 70. What are 15 fives?

6   If I save 2p on each day in March, how much will I save?

7   How many faces has a cuboid?

8   5 added to a number makes 17. What is the number?

9   What fraction of £2 is 50p?

10   Three goals were scored in a football match.
     How many different final scores could there be?

3d

1   86 + 30.

2   Take 75p from £1.10.

3   5×100.

4   Double 49.

5   Nine threes.

6   Two fifths of 50p.

7   Multiply 13 by 10.

8   501 − 3.

9   How many is 2 dozen?

10   19 + 16.

4a

1. 73 – 6.
2. Seven fives.
3. 35 – 8.
4. 43 × 100.
5. 19 + 12.

6. Add 3, 8 and 9.
7. One sixth of 300.
8. Take 8 from 9 plus 3.
9. Ten times fifteen.
10. 38 + 49 = 87. What is 87 – 49?

4b

Copy the diagram.

Use each of the numbers 1 to 9.
Write a number in every circle.

Each line of five numbers
must add up to 23.

Now make lines which total 25.

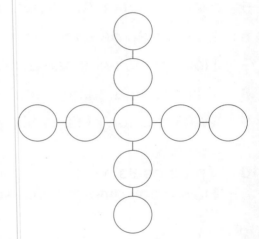

1 2 3 4 5 6 7 8 9

4c

1. 126 – 40.
2. 18 + 14.
3. 36 ÷ 4.
4. 42 minus 9.
5. 5 × □ = 40.

6. One fifth of £2.
7. 11 + 11.
8. Decrease 13 by 6.
9. Divide 3000 by 10.
10. □ ÷ 6 = 6.

Five pin bowling

1   Susan knocked over 13 and 15. What was her total score?

2   Two children each bowled over one pin.
    The difference in their scores was 5. What were they?

3   Tom scored 20. Which pins did he knock over?

4   Aziz left 13 and 15 standing. What was his score?

5   Emma scored 30. Which pins fell down?

6   If Harry had scored 7 more, he would have got 31.
    Which pins fell over?

7   Is it possible to knock down just two pins and score 25?

8   Rupa got 35 with three pins. Which did she knock down?

9   What is the greatest possible score?

10 Mark scored 10 more than Carol.
    They each knocked down two pins. What were their scores?

5a

1	52 − 5.	**6**	48 + 7.
2	250 + 60.	**7**	0 × 10.
3	17 + 19.	**8**	Half of 50.
4	540 ÷ 10.	**9**	Nine fours.
5	3 plus 4 plus 8.	**10**	Two squared.

5b

1   What time was it 10 minutes ago?

2   By what must I multiply 11 to make 110?

3   Write **seven thousand and two** in figures.

4   How many teams of four can 30 children make?

5   How long is it from 2:50 p.m. to 3:10 p.m?

6   Approximately, what is 152 − 98?

7   What is the total length of 4 strips of wood, each 25 cm long?

8   How many children can have
3 pencils each from 17 pencils?

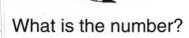

9   If 5 is taken from a number, 17 is left. What is the number?

10   It is 48 miles from Andover to Oxford.
How far is it there and back?

5c

Opposite faces of a dice add up to 7.
These are the top faces. How many spots are touching the table?

1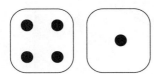

2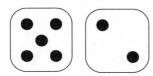

3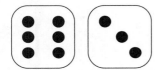

4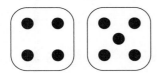

5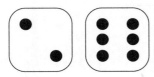

6

7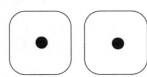

8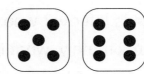

9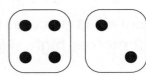

10

5d

1   Double 19.

2   Seven threes.

3   Half of 15.

4   $130 \div 10$.

5   $18 + 13$.

6   $259 - 60$.

7   4×7.

8   $55 \div 5$.

9   One quarter of 100.

10   $43 - 8$.

6a

1. Peter cut two ribbons, each 44 cm long, from 1 metre of ribbon. How much was left?

2. Which divide exactly by three: 18, 19, 20, 21, 22?

3. Which four coins make £1.65?

4. What is this shape called?

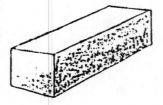

5. Write **seven tenths** as a decimal.

6. What is left over when 29 is divided by 3?

7. Approximately, what is 9×21?

8. How many 5 kg bags can be filled from 36 kg of potatoes?

9. A painting is twice as high as it is wide. It is 2 metres high. How wide is it?

10. How many rectangles can you see altogether?

6b

1. Take 5 from 19 plus 4.
2. Decrease 70 by 4.
3. $7400 \div 10$.
4. $64 - 9$.
5. One sixth of 360.
6. $2 + 9 + 7$.
7. 8×5.
8. Three squared.
9. $18 + 19$.
10. Is 67.1 nearer to 60 or 70?

6c

1	Nine fives.	6	Half of 90.
2	800 ÷ 100.	7	$27 \times 4 = 108$. What is $108 \div 4$?
3	18 + 15.	8	8×4.
4	Four fifths of £1.	9	Divide 28 by 4.
5	71 − 8.	10	One quarter of 1000.

6d

Into the unknown

 S P A C E
5   10   15   20   25

Add up the numbers standing for the letters in each word.

1	APE.	4	PEAS.	7	CAPE.
2	CAP.	5	CASE.	8	EASE.
3	ASS.	6	PASS.	9	PEEPS.

7a

1	89 + 5.	**6**	16 plus 18.
2	2 multiplied by 9.	**7**	Double 37.
3	Five fours.	**8**	40 ÷ 4.
4	3900 ÷ 100.	**9**	Four squared.
5	53 – 6.	**10**	24 divided by 3.

7b

1 A box of crayons cost 37p. What was the change from 50p?

2 What are the next two numbers: 17, 13, 9, 5 …?

3 You have only 50p coins.
How many should you give to pay £2.05?

4 What is the value of the 3 in 4.3?

5 Is this triangle isosceles?

6 How long is it from 3:30 p.m. to 5:15 p.m?

7 8 km is about 5 miles. About how many kilometres is 20 miles?

8 How many days altogether in September and October?

9 Ismat has saved £1.66.
How much more must she save to have £2?

10 A snail crawls 10 cm in 10 minutes.
How far does it crawl in an hour?

7c

1   31 − 4.

2   4 × 9.

3   One fifth of 1 metre.

4   5000 ÷ 100.

5   Add 17 to 18.

6   Eight threes.

7   Half of 3000.

8   5 × □ = 35.

9   Add 500 g and half a kilogram.

10   How many socks in 13 pairs?

7d

Draw five boxes.

Use each of the numbers 1 to 9 once.

Write the numbers in the boxes.

The total in each box must be 9.

Now draw three boxes.

Use the same numbers.

This time, the total in each box must be 15.

Do it in at least three different ways.

1 2 3 4 5 6 7 8 9

8a

1   Write **sixty-nine hundredths** as a decimal.

2   What is next: 18, 22, 26, 30 …?

3   My sister is 3 cm short of 1 metre. How tall is she?

4   How many grams is 1.5 kilograms?

5   Notebooks are 19p each.
    How many can I get for £1.90?

6   How many minutes in 1½ hours?

7   Add together 60 cm and half a metre.

8   How much longer is 20 days than 2 weeks?

9   Twice a number is 4 less than 10. What is the number?

10 How many weeks in a year?

8b

Draw two squares.

Use each of the numbers 1 to 7 once.
Write them in the squares.

The total in the large square must be
three times the total in the small square.

Do it in five different ways.

1 2 3 4 5 6 7

8c

1 4 golf balls fit in a box.
   How many boxes are needed for 17 golf balls?

2 $5 \times 17 = 85$. What is 5×18?

3 How long is the perimeter of a 2 cm by 3 cm rectangle?

4 If each number is the sum of the two before it,
   what are the missing numbers in this pattern?

   $$1, \ \square, \ 4, \ \square, \ \square, \ \square.$$

5 What is the value of the 9 in 0.09?

6 How many edges has a cuboid?

7 It takes me 5 minutes to clean a pair of shoes.
   How many shoes can I clean in 35 minutes?

8 Three quarters of the 400 children at a school are present.
   How many are absent?

9 How many degrees are two right angles?

10 What is this shape called?

8d

1 $9000 \div 10$.

2 $18 + 18$.

3 4 less than 9×4.

4 Seven squared.

5 $92 - 7$.

6 Half of 78.

7 Take 45 minutes from 1 hour.

8 6×4.

9 How many 5p coins make 45p?

10 How many centimetres in 1.5 m?

9a

| Glasgow | | Falkirk | | Linlithgow | | Edinburgh |

10 minutes

A train travels between Glasgow and Edinburgh.

From Falkirk to Linlithgow takes 10 minutes.

a. Copy and complete the timetable for the 09:00 and 09:40 trains.

Glasgow	09:00	09:40
Falkirk	09:15	
Linlithgow		
Edinburgh		10:35

b. How long does it take from Linlithgow to Edinburgh?

c. The train waits at Edinburgh for 15 minutes before going back to Glasgow.

Copy and complete the timetable for the two return journeys.

Edinburgh		
Linlithgow		
Falkirk		
Glasgow		

9b

Imagine 20 cubes arranged in 3 towers.

The first tower has 8 more than the second.
The second has half as many as the third.

How many cubes in each tower?

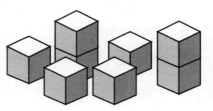

9c

1   How many buns at 30p each can you get for £3?
2   What is the total length of four 2.5 m ropes?
3   What is the least number of coins needed to make £1.43?
4   Add 500 g to one quarter of a kilogram.
5   The side of a square is 10 cm. How long is its perimeter?
6   How much more than 300 ml is half a litre?
7   How many right angles make 270°?
8   Roughly, what is 11 × 51?
9   What is this shape called?
10 Write all the factors of 15.

9d

1	Five sixes.	6	Eight squared.
2	13 + 19.	7	12 ÷ 4.
3	65 − 9.	8	Is 25 a multiple of 3?
4	Double 15.	9	Take three tenths from 1.
5	Which is more: 0.8 or 1.2?	10	Three quarters of 1000.

10a

1 15 + 16.

2 34 − 8.

3 Nine sixes.

4 Which is less: 2.5 or 5.2?

5 $4 \times \square = 20$.

6 Two fifths of 500.

7 17 ÷ 2.

8 Write **0.3** in words.

9 Add 0.4 to 0.5.

10 How many fives in 35?

10b

1 Is this triangle equilateral?

2 Write **three hundredths** as a decimal.

3 What is the cost of 250 g of tea at £2 per kilogram?

4 I can walk 3 km in 45 minutes.
   How long does it take to walk 6 km?

5 How long is it from 9:30 a.m. to 11:05 a.m.?

6 It is Monday, March 29th. What date is next Friday?

7 2 metres of string is cut into 10 equal pieces.
   How long is each piece?

8 If 6 eggs fill one box, how many boxes will 25 eggs fill?

9 Mum spent 1½ hours gardening.
   She started at 2:40 p.m. What time did she finish?

10 What number have these in common:
   October, an octopus and an octagon?

Magic curves

Copy the diagram.

Use a different colour for each of the three curves.

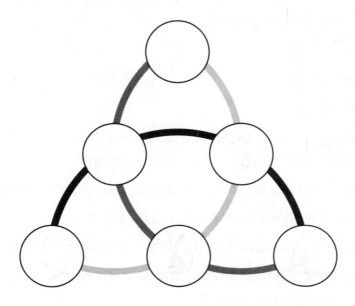

Use each of the numbers 1 to 6. Write one number in each circle.

The sum of the numbers on each curve must be 14.

1	What is 0.75 as a fraction?	**6**	Take 29 from 50.
2	$4 \times \Box = 32$.	**7**	Two thirds of 90.
3	$54 - 7$.	**8**	Subtract three fifths from 1.
4	Square five.	**9**	5 plus 17.
5	$21 \div 2$.	**10**	How many nines in 45?

1   How long is it from 18:55 to 19:10?

2   Egg boxes hold 6 eggs.
    How many boxes are needed for 15 eggs?

3   What is this solid called?

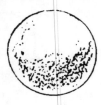

4   I choose a number, double it, then subtract 4.
    The answer is 6. What was the number?

5   To reach 0, how many times must 3 be subtracted from 18?

6   What two numbers come next: 20, 15, 10, 5 …?

7   The edge of a square is 2 metres. What is its area?

8   How much do 28 bananas cost at 7 for 50p?

9   Stamps are £20 for 100.
    What is the price of one stamp?

10 How many triangles
    can you see altogether?

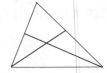

1   $100 - 76$.

2   If $\blacklozenge \times \blacklozenge = 49$, what is $\blacklozenge$?

3   One quarter of 13.

4   $12 - \square - 2 = 4$.

5   $81 - 6$.

6   How many litres is 1500 ml?

7   $16 + 17$.

8   Square 9.

9   100×10.

10 Approximately, what is $39 + 58$?

1 One third of 24.

2 40 − 8.

3 Six squared.

4 65 − 7.

5 $3 \times \square = 27$.

6 $\square − 3 − 2 = 6$.

7 $50 \div 5$.

8 One quarter of 5.

9 15 + 7.

10 Twelve threes plus one.

11d

Copy the diagram.

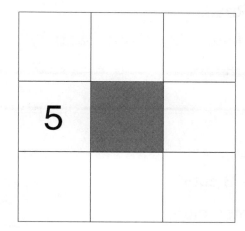

Use each of the numbers 1 to 8.
Write one number in every box.
5 is already in place.

Each side of the square must add up to 12.

Now do it so that each side adds up to 15.

1 2 3 4 5 6 7 8

12a

Birmingham New Street	0940	1005	1105	1235
Birmingham International	0950	1015	1115	1245
Coventry	1010	1030	1130	1300
Leamington Spa	1025	....	1145	1315
Banbury	1045	....	1205	....
Oxford	1105	1120	1225	1355
Reading	1130	1155	1250	1425

How long does the fastest train take between :

a. Birmingham New Street and Reading;

b. Coventry and Oxford;

c. Oxford and Reading;

d. Birmingham International and Banbury?

12b

Imagine a solid 3 × 3 cube.

The outside is painted blue.

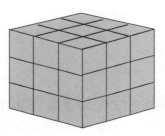

How many of the small cubes have:

a. 3 blue faces;

b. 2 blue faces;

c. 1 blue face;

d. 0 blue faces?

12c

1. How many degrees between the hands of this clock?

2. How many halves is 8.5?

3. How much for 15 lollies at 3p each?

4. A man and a child travelled on a train for £30.
   The child's ticket was half the full fare.
   What did the man's ticket cost?

5. How many days altogether in April, May and June?

6. How many faces has a triangular prism?

7. The area of a rectangle is 12 cm².
   Its width is 2 cm. What is its length?

8. How many 200 g packets can be made from 1 kg of sugar?

9. Dad put his curry in the oven at 7.15 p.m.
   It took 35 minutes to cook.
   When was it ready?

10. How much is this altogether?

12d

1. Eight sixes.
2. 42 − 8.
3. One tenth of 5.
4. 21 ÷ 3.
5. Add 19 to 15.

6. $3 \times \square + 1 = 19$
7. 19 ÷ 2.
8. Three fours plus nine.
9. 21 ÷ 5.
10. How many fives in 60?

Sports Centre

These are the prices of the activities at the Sports Centre.

	Adult	Child
Swimming	1.50	0.80
Table tennis	0.50	0.30
Squash	1.10	0.50
Putting	1.20	0.60
Skating	1.00	0.70
Cycling	1.40	0.40
Badminton	1.00	0.60

1   What does it cost for a child to play badminton?

2   What does it cost for an adult and two children to skate?

3   Four children played table tennis. What did it cost?

4   How much more is it for an adult to swim than a child?

5   For which sport is the price for an adult double that for a child?

6   Two children went swimming.
    How much change did they get from £2?

7   Is it cheaper for an adult and a child to skate or to cycle?

8   How much less did it cost two children to play squash than two adults?

9   Mum did a different activity each day of the week.
    What did it cost her?

10 Mum, Dad and the twins played badminton.
    How much change was there from £5?

1 Twice seventeen.	**6** Ten squared.
2 $25 + 75$.	**7** $6 + 5 + \square = 19$.
3 $53 - 9$.	**8** How many kilograms is 750 g?
4 Double three quarters.	**9** 20 more than 55.
5 Roughly, what is $200 \div 9$?	**10** From 16, take 6 plus 3.

Copy and complete this addition table.

+		8	3		6
	8			9	
2			5		
	9		8		
					9

1 Half of one third.	**6** How many 5p coins make 35p?
2 20×0.	**7** Double 16.
3 $63 - 8$.	**8** How many metres in 1 kilometre?
4 Increase 42 by 20.	**9** $100 - 49$.
5 $5000 \div 10$.	**10** How many nines make 18?

14a

1	Increase 16 by 14.	**6**	Approximately, what is 11×19?
2	Eleven threes.	**7**	Double 150.
3	Add 5, 9 and 4.	**8**	$41 - 8 - \square = 29$.
4	$83 + 7$.	**9**	$250 \div 50$.
5	$74 - 6$.	**10**	One hundredth of 6 metres.

14b

1 It is 10 minutes to six. What time was it 25 minutes ago?

2 What must be added to 14 to make 26?

3 Crisps cost 19p a packet.
If you buy as many packets as you can with £1,
what change do you get?

4 If each number is the sum of the two before it,
what are the missing numbers in this pattern?

$$3, \square, \square, 7, \square, \square.$$

5 $15 \times 6 = 90$. What is 15×3?

6 $1\frac{1}{2}$ litres of milk costs 90p. What does one litre cost?

7 Find the product of 7, 6 and 2.

8 I think of a number, add 5, and double that.
The answer is 18. What number did I think of?

9 How many quarters in seven wholes?

10 The area of a square is $36\,cm^2$.
What is the length of one edge?

$$36\,cm^2$$

Magic star

The numbers along each line of this magic star add up to 30.

What do the letters **MAGIC** stand for?

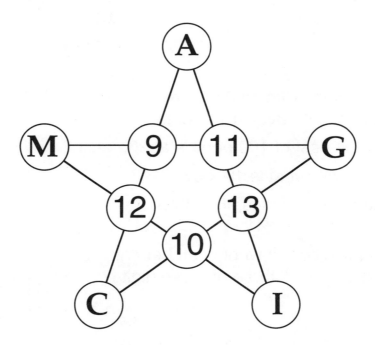

1   Decrease 71 by 9.

2   Eleven fours.

3   48 + 7.

4   $\square \times 3 = 36$.

5   $\square + 6 + 8 = 21$.

6   17 + 13.

7   Half the sum of 14 and 10.

8   90 − 4.

9   Roughly, what is 299 ÷ 9?

10   41 ÷ 4.

15a

1	18 + 12.	**6**	Eleven fives.
2	14 ÷ 4.	**7**	52 – 6.
3	Half of 1.5.	**8**	15 + □ = 29.
4	(9 × 4) + 3.	**9**	Find the product of 2, 3 and 4.
5	100 – 90.	**10**	How many litres is 700 ml?

15b

1 A train travels 24 km in 8 minutes.
How far does it travel in 1 minute?

2 What is the cost of 100 pencils at 20p each?

3 If 16 × 3 = 48, what is 16 × 6?

4 Approximately, what is 96 + 352?

5 How many different whole number can
you make from all three of these digits?

6 If the temperature has risen by 7 °C from –5 °C, what is it now?

7 It is Friday, 27th July. What date is next Thursday?

8 Jane is 1.32 m tall. Emma is 4 cm taller. How tall is Emma?

9 How many seconds is 1½ minutes?

10 A bag of 15 coins is worth £1.05.
There are only 10p and 1p coins in the bag.
How many 10p coins are there?

1	Seven sixes.	**6**	One squared.
2	$12 + \square + 6 = 25$	**7**	$45 + 8$.
3	$10 \times 10 \times 10$.	**8**	Find the sum of 5, 9 and 8.
4	Half of one quarter.	**9**	Approximately, what is 29×31?
5	$19 + 11$.	**10**	$93 - 5$.

Magic triangles

Copy the diagram.

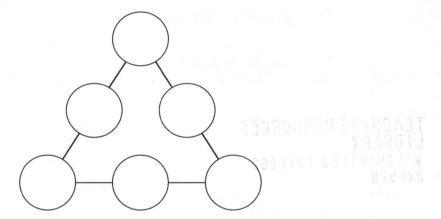

Use each of the numbers 1, 2, 3, 4, 6 and 7.
Write one number in every circle.

Each side of the triangle must add up to 11.

Now do it so that each side adds up to 12.

1 2 3 4 and 6 7

Published by the Press Syndicate of the University of Cambridge
The Pitt Building, Trumpington Street, Cambridge CB2 1RP
40 West 20th Street, New York, NY 10011–4211, USA
10 Stamford Road, Oakleigh, Melbourne 3166, Australia

© Cambridge University Press 1994

First published 1994
Third printing 1996

Printed in Great Britain by Scotprint Ltd, Musselburgh

A catalogue record for this book is available from the British Library.

ISBN 0 521 48553 3   paperback

Cover illustration by Tony Hall
Cartoons by Tim Sell

Notice to teachers
It is illegal to reproduce any part of this work in material form
(including photocopying and electronic storage) except under the
following circumstances:
(i)   where you are abiding by a licence granted to your school by
      the Copyright Licensing Agency;
(ii)   where no such licence exists, or where you wish to exceed the
      terms of a licence, and you have gained the written permission
      of Cambridge University Press;
(iii) where you are allowed to reproduce without permission under
      the provisions of Chapter 3 of the Copyright, Designs and
      Patents Act 1988.